Breeze In The Water

Alexandra V. Tanygina

Dacha Press © 2019

ISBN: 0-646-80124-4
ISBN-13: 978-0-646-80124-7

Cover design by Olga Davletshina & Alexandra Tanygina
Illustrations by Maria Tanygina & Alexandra Tanygina
French translation for "Marriage d'Amour" by Marème Diop
Author photo by Oliver Minett

To John, I finally finished it.

And to anyone who is currently in pain.

CONTENTS

CONTENTS

CONTENTS

CONTENTS

CONTENTS

CONTENTS

CONTENTS

The Introduction

While the meat of this book was finished years ago, it took me so long to compile and edit this book and even longer to write/re-write even the simplest of introductions. I am a strong believer that things happen for a reason and that the delay in my writing happened for a reason. This book was written over years on and off throughout my growing and experiences as a young adult, which I still am. There are many things I just do not relate to any longer and many things that I rediscover upon reading my first collection again; thoughts and feelings that I may have buried deeper in my mind. But I am glad I wrote down what I could; this book is a journey, a poetic recounting on a part of my life.

'Breeze In The Water' is a phrase that just stuck in my mind, never truly unravelling itself till the present. Our lives are an endless ocean of experiences and every experience is just a small flicker in time, like a snapshot hastily taken whilst on the run to something we deemed more important at that time.

I hope that whoever reads this book makes sense of whatever my words are trying to say. I hope that it helps you develop and grow on your own journey in the vast ocean of life, and to learn from every breeze.

Everyone has a story, here is a part of mine.

A special thank you to my friends and family past and present, I thank you all for the love and support over the years.

An additional thank you to myself for having the strength, courage and ambition to work hard to achieve my dreams.

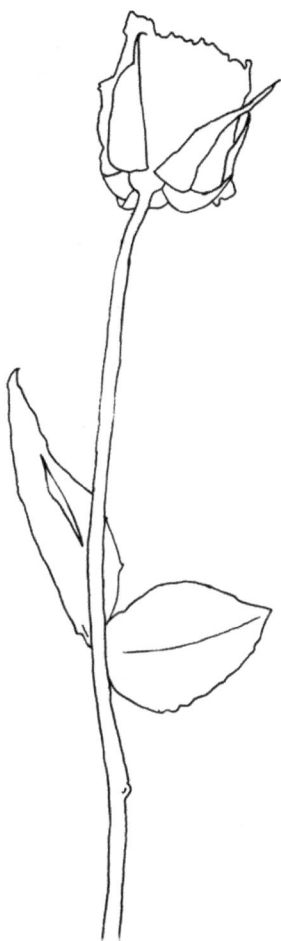

Crimson Pool

Every passing time, her trust, her shield is chiseled away and she begins to weaken, though like a crab she builds a new shell a new shield to protect her from the ones with the charming faces and the soothing words that smoothly roll of their tongues.

Every passing time, she finds someone new to devote her love and energy and every passing time the flower that was once blooming begins to rot, she finds herself with a bouquet of dead roses.

Though every passing time, a bud begins to bloom and bloom and bloom, like the crab security is what she yearns and this charming face with soothing words that smoothly roll of his tongue begins to shield her, protect her and become her new shell.

A flower is only finite, it is a life and with life always comes death.

From first breath until the end, a journey of time and experience.

Set alight she begins to burn, her emotions like a terrifying wave, she knows that that day must happen.

So, she begins to close the curtain on the man she once loved, she tries to forget and tries to forget.

She bleeds from her eyes, and bleeds from inside, a crimson pool beneath her.

*The insecure man grovels before me in total despair
uttering nonsense attempting to fix what he cannot repair.*

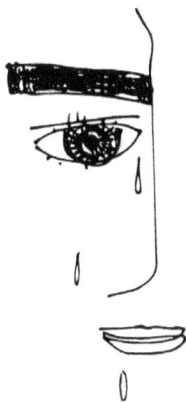

Define – Love

Love, a word that resonates with many,
a word so strong that befalls even the bravest of armies,
a word, one word that will cripple any being,
a power so revered, a light that cannot be feared.

Love, a feeling echoed by the masses, a feeling that
can crush the spirit of the many beings that held it,
a feeling, the only feeling that can completely disarray
you, a power so important, that without, our lives are
shortened.

Crush

Oh my my, how did this happen?
I've got a crush on you.

I sleep at night and dream about you
seeing stars, most thoughts elude my head.
I've not a clue of where I would be in my life, without
you.

Please love me, kindly, deeply and slow,
akin to the moon and the waves she ebbs and flows
under the night sky watching those eyes.

Laying in your arms a feeling so calm,
or in my bed listening to the rain drip on my roof.

Oh my my, how did this happen?
I've got a crush on you.

Tell me.

Oh honey, honey, where did you go last night?
Why can't you reveal to me all that you hide?
Do you fear that what you may have done is wrong?
Or are you scared of the repercussions that might be strong?

Oh honey, honey, tell me where you were,
I cannot appease you, my heart is sore,
I whinge and cry like a baby to your delight,
I called all night, please let's not fight.

Oh honey, honey, tell me.

I miss your love so much
and I want to be loved like that again,
make it the same as you did with me way back then.

<u>Those Summer Nights</u>

Long gone those summer nights,
by the pond under the pale moonlight,
a little story that we once had,
watching pups and getting mad.

The fish we fed had all died out,
the ducks and trees their life in doubt,
our once warm night, became so cold
just like this tale that is being told.

Misunderstood by one another,
love never truly felt by each other,
now why are my stories all so grim?
a question pondered, was the answer him?

With my mind led far astray
I ask myself, do I go out and play?
Though that night I was entranced,
we rolled down hills whilst we danced.

In the end you watched me go,
kissed my cheek, your eyes slow
the light dimming, shone a wonder,
the gift of young love given to another.

Untitled #1

The clouds a pinkish gray,
a perfectly mixed paint gradient carefully
placed on a blank sheet of azure paper.

Unconvinced of dawn or dusk
a delirious haze so innocent,
simply impossible to convict.

Love In The City

Staring deep into my eyes, you wonder why I'm
disguised, attempting to enter my soul my walls begin to
crumble.

You hold my hand whilst we walk through the rain
it sure is getting cold out here, but I know it's not in vain.

We enter your domain, an internal fire ignites
Inside your warm arms, the rest of my body is set alight.

Your reach is far, strong and wide,
domineering with nowhere to hide.

My mind consumed by weakness and fright
but my body yearns for more, this precious delight.

My heart has fallen to the gravest of men
Love In The City is not how it should end.

A moment in the Bay

Looking out the window
Seeing the blue blanket, hearing the white flies
Humans and canines, I enjoyed those moments, but why?

When the blue blankets turns navy,
and the white flies become black
I feel at home and I feel so safe,
this breeze I dare not ever forget.

And then I left him,
because I could no longer bare
A life in a cage without spark nor flare.

Untitled #2

Silence, one word,
silence, two words,
You barely mutter a breath.

I constantly wonder, what is in your head.
I fear that you may be closed off from me,
my heart aches because I know you want to be set free.

I open my cage,
I open my heart,
I open my soul,
withering inside me I am all alone.

Please do not fear me, I am loving, I am warm
but if you cannot see this I will be taken with the storm.

Turn your back to me and I will do as you,
don't underestimate my kindness,
A crimson red heart can turn to blue.

*He kissed my forehead and glanced at me one last time,
then walked out the door without even saying goodbye.*

<u>Smoking Men</u>

The man waltzing right next to me,
chuffing on his death stick,
the scent triggering a
nostalgia of a past lover.

I recalled a day when we were fighting,
I'm so sick of these smoking men.

Falling from the Pedestal

In his eyes was his own gleaming demise
of how he once was and for how he was once known.

A gallant stallion fearing the mouse,
writhing uncontrollably his destiny already sewn.

But in the end the sufferable suffer,
so he walked away and became another.

He could neither help, nor was he willing
to deal with his reality; a sin like no other.

My heart falls with the flowers
knowing that you've moved on,

even though the reason you left
was entirely my own.

Alexandra V. Tanygina

Prey

Numbness a feeling of nothingness,
insecurity creeping.

A demon I thought I vanquished
but apparently only quelled.

The thousand daggers that I flung barely
scrapping the shell of this horrific monster.

What must I do to separate myself from you?

Your claws no longer protect and only dig deeper into my
flesh.

The puncture wounds getting closer and closer to my
ever-beating heart.

You prowl with your fanged companions, stalking and
waiting patiently
until a moment materializes.

Bang! The scent of gunpowder,

and there on a field of white snow, lay a gun-shot
swallow.

Untitled #3

Soft and so warm like a mellowed heart
kind and honest, death do us part.
A romance filled with joy and love,
a beauty so pure like a crystal white dove.

An essence betrothed to one another,
cradled in your arms just like your mother's,
rest your head my young sweet thing
quite unsure of what tomorrow will bring.

All your thoughts will calm and hollow
now no longer will you sleep with sorrow,
lay beneath the velvet night
sleeping quietly out of sight.

<u>One of Us</u>

Oh I know my love, how easy it is to get lost and
to wonder in fear of how much life would cost.

I know that you'd much rather spend your time playing
video games, but apparently being an adult is about using
our brains.

One of us has to be responsible,
one of us has to ensure our lives are sensible,

And I understand that you might only want to live in
comfort, but if we don't act know there will only be
discomfort.

So I beg you my love, please figure something out,
I'm sick and tired of messing about.

I want our lives to synchronise
so please let's find a compromise.

And though he left for his own journey,
I remembered the times we had fondly.

<u>Untitled #4</u>

I mean you no malice,
I mean you no harm,
but why when I ask a question
you dare not disarm?

I find you annoying,
I find you hurtful,
your words mean nothing,
like a snake that is hateful.

I wish to love you,
and I wish to fight,
I try to believe you
but it's all in hindsight.

You make me weak,
as I make you strong,
I love you so much,
but you make it feel wrong.

A recluse I've become
believing your words,
wishing you'd have never come
I hope you mean me no harm.

Dreams & Wishes

Alas the tale comes to an end,
two people, no compromise.

The veil of trust slowly teared
to a point where it can no longer be
sewn back together.

A broken record player no longer replaying itself,
destroyed beyond repair, no fix or refurbishment possible.

The band-aids falling off as soon as they're laid
everything has an expiration date and
all those feelings dissipate.

Returning to a realm that they never left,
becoming just dreams and wishes.

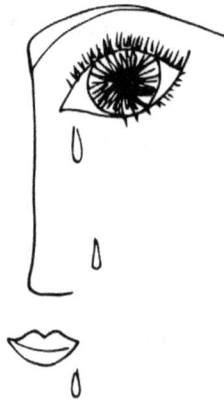

A ploy played by the cruel and the wicked
forced upon the foolish and the weak.
A poisoning of the mind, love is lie.

Empathy

I feel as though when I speak to another being,
my energy is immediately depleted.

My empathy was whole and unconditional,
but now it all feels too exhausting.

I give advice that they ask for in hopes that they will
change, I share my advice, but it seems like it's all in
vain.

Now I wonder why and when this happened,
though it doesn't bother me so much.

People just want to be heard and listened,
but I grow tired even giving them that much.

Labour

I'm tired of being your therapist,
even though you've never sent me a pay cheque.

I'm tired of being your mother,
even though I never birthed you myself.

and now,

I'm tired of being your lover,
even though you never loved me back.

So please just go and sort out your issues,
and leave me in the black.

I'll be alright

I'll be alright as long as the light
is shining from the full moon.

I'll be alright and safe within sight
as long as my heart is with you.

I'll be alright because I know what is right
God's plan is simply my tool.

I'll be alright as long as the light
is shining from the full moon.

Oh Luna

Oh Luna, Oh Luna
How mighty, might you be?
You push and pull
Are you crying? Would you like to be set free?

Oh Luna, Oh Luna
How patient might you be?
You watch and sigh
Are you angry? Please don't cry.

9:26PM

*I sit here contemplating, the moon turned yellow tonight,
I look in front of me, but only your shadows
remains.*

Owl

Crying in the night
an owl with sore eyes
a foreseen dilemma, predicted.

Holding herself in the bed they once shared,
rustled feathers fluttering through the room,
the calmest breeze becoming so disruptive,

Moved by the sounds of her mother's callings
flapping her tiny wings pursuing the flight,
but the pain far too strong for her delicate body to bare.

This pale white owl no longer mourning,
gently blanketed, the sun beginning to rise,
hush your mind it's time to rest.

Crux

The night beholds me your five bright eyes,
a remembrance of my new home, a lust I disguise.
Wishing upon a star, for dreams that may not come true,
holding back tears, for a future that may not be due.

I see now only four bright eyes,
why did one leave? Were my eyes all lies?
My body swallowed, by my own dark mind
now looking deep inside I'm trying to find,

A way to live in this cruel world,
a way to have myself preserved,
one more star now leaves the four
only three now left to adore.

The light comes creeping from the east,
closing eyes as it's pleased.
Dawn is here and will not go
for some hours it will show.

Until nightfall strikes again
I bid you adieu,
my dear old friend.

<u>Lonely</u>

Feeling so down, unheld and forgotten
up came the high and now comes the low,
turbulent emotions, unaware of control
possessed by her sadness with no future to hold.

Yearning for a message or call
a sign to know what beckons beyond.
Dark and cold in her empty room
she struggles, unable to find warmth.

Next to the heater she sits,
the machine barely working.
Grasping for sanity a mental challenge ensuing,
curtains waving from afar, glooming light from the
windows.

Feelings swell inside her that she does not like,
looking from within attempting to discern what is right.
Unable to debate as to what she must do next
this poor young soul is truly stuck in her head.

Dance with the Devil

An ode with our dance to the heathens below,
Violins and Cellos playing for all,
The theatre seats as empty as before,
Our love not hidden, we scream "Encore!".

A passion so strong that ignites thin air,
a flame so hot, it burns all whom aware,
So forbidden is the Incubi's touch,
that when had, once is never enough.

And now our dance has come to an end
left weak and brittle, no one there to tend
a bruised and battered lifeless shell,
screams of horror unable to quell.

The love affair that seemed too brief
Eternal damnation, there is no relief,
so now brave heroin I heed you this warning,
a *Dance with the Devil* only ends with mourning.

Define – Paranoia

Paranoia, a mind irrational,
knowing the truth yet disregarding it completely.

A delicately concocted mix of intuition and delusion,
a poison that feeds the mind.

Paranoia, a mind neglecting
the absolute truth in front of our eyes.

A poised condition, unchallenged to its rule.

Untitled #5

Part of me inflects onto a part of you
every soul I pass, I leave a piece in you.

Deep inside you lead no recollection,
of what was past or whom was in your collection.

A mind that wallows, depressed and alone
recognizing fault is your own resurrection.

Walking the long walk all alone,
you get tired you grow old

and on your bed you continue to wallow,
reflecting on your life, your life is hollow.

No love, no art, no beauty, no gold
a life so lonesome, the world will grow old.

Adrift

A feeling of loss that is all encompassing
I am helpless to my own thoughts.

I drift along in the dark waters,
bright like a comet in the cosmos.

I sing a song that no one can hear,
floating through the endless.

Mindless of the times,
beginnings with new rhymes.

A feeling of loss that is just destructive
I am helpless to minds above it.

Even though I try to distance myself
you cannot help but fly back to me,

addicted you are,

like the bees and their lavender.

<u>Declination</u>

Finally awaking after many sleepless nights, trying to make sense of the past days.

Confusion leads you to more, stuck in a cycle of comprehension that is not comprehensible.

Your mind weaker, your body drained, and your soul exhausted, you look to the past and recollect how you once were and begin to think if that is the only path for you which you can take.

Tripping down the spiral staircase of delirium, accelerating at every flight, seduced into a constant state of nostalgia and melancholy.

Quickly declining into an abyss that was your former devolved inexperienced person, ignoring your soul and only seeking the desires of your physical realm, you think of what was and what is to come, the future uncertain and far from bright, fear takes control and a once powerful entity becomes akin to primitivity.

Untitled #6

The typicality of the atypical, a difference born, a
difference assumed.

Opposing thoughts, opposing ideals, inexplicitly detailed,
down to the fibre of being.

A stroll through the maze of life, new dangers await, new
love awaits.

Constructions of time, we weep and laugh, a theme-park
rollercoaster;

a true simulation of our time on this plane.

Alexandra V. Tanygina

String

Rolling and rolling down the stairs,
a ball of string unfolds, it dares,

Strength it gathers, gone down each flight,
it doesn't hesitate, it's not in fright,

The smaller it gets the less it is known,
seemingly invisible, down to the bone,

Now we wonder why the ball is missing,
frantically calling, you hear it hissing,

This once big ball is now so little,
in fear we lose, our path is brittle.

Path

I lost my way, through a million distractions,
shoved off my path, by your million little actions.

It felt like more than a week, it was only a few days
the driver of your life was being replaced.

Gone down the off the beaten track,
bumping corner to corner worrying of how I'll get back.

I take the wheel and take back my life for If I let
my impulses live my life would be without a path.

<u>Nostalgia</u>

A nostalgia so painful, a longing for the past, a childhood
well loved, memories so fond that I dare not ever forget
them.

I weep to the music that the old men played
in their cafes on the cobbled stone streets of Paris,
a century before my current depiction.

A dance in the snow, the making men and angels
a childhood so treasured, the past could not ever foresee.

An innocence so greatly lost, a disparity of ones
emotions, laying in my casket for the night, held by the
one I hold dear.

No sense nor calm, a tight grip is all that is needed.

Endless rivers from the gates to my soul remembering all,
wishing that I was there safely, back in my cocoon of
youth.

Strings of silk will guide me there whenever hope is lost,
I speak to you young child, remember me and I'll
remember you.

<u>Still Healing</u>

There was a time that I suffered almost daily
sticking band-aids on a broken cup with many holes,

Water dripping from the cracks, alone to fix for myself
but I know I don't feel that bad anymore.

There's a box inside my head,

That keeps away all the traumas and hides all the pain
from the people that love me and the people that stay
away,

and I am sorry for my deception but I just cannot be open
always, because I am still healing from all those dark
days.

Reassurance

Sick and tired of feeling sick and tired of feeling sick and tired of feeling sick and tired, a recurring feeling, a cycle of insanity that simply drives me insane.

I cursed myself when I was younger, holding no love for myself I drove myself to a pit of despair. What I felt during those long days are feelings I would not wish upon anyone. I regret nothing, as I've learnt so much, but none the less crawling out of that pit was a disaster.

Ending that cycle had to come from me, the love I held for life outweighed the love I held for myself, yet that was enough to keep this engine running, breaking the chains, I felt so free, no longer tormented by those demons.

Victory could not be called so early though, as those demons were slain, arose new ones, stronger, harsher and deadlier, more willing to end me than the ones that came before and daily I still fight them.

I will be the last one standing, you watch.

Moments

On a mid-winter night as she brushed her legs onto the
fresh velvet linens, she lay there, in bed peacefully
nodding into another land.

A beautiful tune plays from her modern-age gramophone,
melodic and so hypnotizing, a true moment of bliss.

Moments she doesn't have all too often, moments she
forgets about, moments she doesn't allow herself except
this one time.

This one time she wrote it down and so she lay there,
melting into her coffin of dreams, her mind finally at
ease.

Here he stands right before the lake,
the man that doesn't understand love or fate.

Untitled #7

In the times of yesteryear when the trees swung just right,
the shadows belonging to the unknown alleviating
insight.

A passion so strong,
a feeling so wrong,
two little lovebirds chirping at the brink of dawn.

Of the future, past and present
Of what's gone what was pleasant,
a lullaby sung to the ones with hearts all alone.

The wind chimes in,

The lady swindles, the man improves
his scheme of love with many moves.

Observations do occur,
a million thoughts,
become a blur.

Frequenting the nightly realm,
returning home right by that elm.

In the times of yesteryear when the trees swung just right,
the light belonging to the unknown alleviated fright.

<u>Lemons</u>

When life gifted me lemons,
I planted trees and the fruits
that it bore saved me.

When life gifted me lemons,
I planted trees and the fruits
that it bore no longer tormented me.

Canvas

The arrival of an easel, a fresh canvas to paint anew.

Long gone a tale of dread and darkness, the light just shining through.

Fixation on the events of yesteryear the mind begins to swallow.

Carbon black paint and giant brush strokes envelopes whilst we wallow.

Yet still inside you know what's right and lead your heart in that direction.

You follow him, you follower her though regardless your path is in correction.

The easel stands, the canvas awaits; a new artist to sit in front of it and paint.

Birthday (July 4)

It's my Birthday. Tears from my eyes for a life already long lived, a serene feeling of hope and excitement for the future that I will hold, an understanding of myself and what is beyond.

Feelings I hold so close and dear, a love for the world so strong without fear, moments that are so surreal, I question, can this all be real? Millenia of life has brought me to this point, what's past and present, souls that traversed a terrain so harsh yet pleasant the pain I've carried no longer resent.

A love so pure I'm truly grateful, for health and healing my mind now helpful, a peace so foreign yet understood, we are all one and same, my brethren should now focus on the world beyond, love, health and healing my one wish because our world is threatened by the hatred above, so hold on tight to those you deem dear and those that you love, forgive and love there is nothing to fear I can promise you that, let yourself and others shine, because the love you hold is your divine, the differences that you have are just fantasies, we all came from one place with such great bounties, a cure for the world is a dream I entail so please without fail, just this once, promise me to be grateful it's sad to see the world so hateful.

<u>Friends & Art</u>

The further they are from the reaches of day
the less they have in their opinion or sway.

To do the thing that you most love gives you power
and to be a part of a group or place that holds you dear
with friends around you shouting cheers.

Us humans love to feel like we are a part
of something greater, when we make our art.

<u>Marriage d'Amour</u>

L'amour, une chose fantaisiste
Love, a whimsical thing

*Pensé pour être compris par les masses, mais mal
compris par tous*
Thought to be understood by the masses, yet
misunderstood by all

Une union de deux personnes, amoureuses
A union of two people, in love

Évident en un jour, une semaine, un mois, une année
Known within a day, a week, a month, a year

Provenance incertaine, on sait seulement qu'il est là
Unknown to whence it happens, it's simply just does

Un bel arrangement, un mariage d'amour
A beautiful arrangement, a marriage of love.

Your love anchored my heart
to the depths of the seas.

Untitled #8

He smiles at the moon the way he smiles at the sun,
a whispering glare beseeched and only seen by the one.

He takes his journey quite afar, chasing vixens and liars
this gallant tale is not so new, a tale of man becoming
two.

A being so brave, strong in and out, he fell in love
without a doubt.

Her beauty incomparable to none, a goddess that has
already won.

Like a mystic from the skies, an angel from the lies
She skated towards him as he was begging for more.

But like the tale of Devil too much of anything you
become disheveled,

so when he reached his final destination, he found himself
within reflection.

Chasing what he thought was love, believing in the Gods
above.

A kiss of death had marked his journey, in the end he
could only beg for mercy.

The Stars In Cancer

The sound of the waves crashing,
from the beach not too far from home.

Heard over miles of oceanic road,
beautifully symphonic and all alone.

A gloomy storm will soon ensue,
a smile from the earth will soon subdue.

Your body resting, floating in an abyss
with only dark waters to hold you towards peace.

As the veil of black glitter swallows the day
the eyes shut tight, the twinkling lights will stay.

Remember now young one when you feel all alone,
look to *The Stars In Cancer* they shall guide you towards
home.

I stand on the pier, drenched by the rain
hoping that what you just said was all in vain.

<u>Mother</u>

The fear in my heart of my mother's lost beat,
I weep endlessly my soul missing a piece.

A loss so dear and great, my mind will never shake,
an anger I've never felt, a blanket coated and baked.

A theatre play, a shield to protect my days,
endearing yet concealing a reality that must be raised.

I look to the stars in search of hope,
forever in my heart she will not go.

Gaia

Life is full of uncertainties, the only predictable thing about life is beauty.

When you lay on the grass staring at the light blue sky, the scent of summer, the songs the birds sing, the sounds mother nature makes, when she continues on and on with what she has been doing for oh so long.

Even when the sun is no longer there, she doesn't rest, when you stare in to the deep navy sky, you see the eyes that have her for billions of years, and when you feel alone, empathise with her, for she has not a soul to comfort her or cradle her in her time of need.

When the winds turn from warm to cold, there is still beauty, the grey cloudy skies, so unique, never the same shade of grey, the rain, the tears the clouds cry, not necessarily the tears of sadness but tears of hope, as once the rain stops, life begins to blossom once more.

There is reason why our species has existed for such a long time; she allowed it. Allowed us to evolve and continue living and moulding into the

species we are today, this thought could simply
be one of arrogance, yet the thought is still one
that is calming and full of warmth.

We are now a species that is more powerful than
our own parent.

Life is beautiful not just individually but as a
whole. It is persistent and diligent, it is the only
certainty available to us.

She will always love us, a non-detachable like a
Mother and her offspring, and even when we no
longer lover her and caused her death, in the
beyond she will continue to love us.

Now is now and then is then just lay and listen to
the music our siblings sing to us.

We must remind ourselves, that life is the one certainty
and it is the one beauty.

As autumn comes and the leaves turn red
I think of you, in the comfort of my own bed.

It's okay

It's okay if you don't like me
or dislike the things I do,

because the things that make my happy
are the things that you argue,

and though you see the bright canopies
of my weathered life and soul,

You see no reason to forgive
or let a being have console,

that's the saddest tale of all,
the inability to absolve at all.

Untitled #9

Feeling so unfamiliar with you, I've known you for so long, why do we feel so distant whilst I'm right in your arms?

Where is your head? Where is your heart?
Tell me your fears and tell me who you love,

I'll try not to judge, but you can't blame me
for what I hear is what I see.

My Body

My body has problems,
that only you seem to find,
that only you seem to take issue with.

My body has problems,
that only you like to care for,
that only you like to insult.

My body has problems,
because you don't like it,
because you don't feel ownership over it.

My body has problems,
because you won't ever love it,
but it's not for you to care, like or love.

Withheld

As I glanced at my own reflection, past the day that I lost my own way, what the woman saw was a woman in awe, of the things she accomplished in only 21 years of her life.

She walks tall with her shoulders propped up like a skyscraper, impregnable to fall and along she marches across the battlefield that is her life.

The warzone torn, like the many worn out men that tried to besiege her, and a remembrance is held almost every day for those very same men that didn't believe in her.

They tried with all their might to belittle her with spite, but those taunts could not fault the open heart within her.

She waited patiently until her chariot arrived, boarding like a Queen and leaving ever so wise.

Now you might wonder what happened to all those men that the horses trampled? Well they were left there, their lives were gambled.

So Is there some kind of lesson to be learnt? Yes for those who hinder progress through insecurity or ego, will find themselves lonely with nowhere to go, they'll seek a new form to indulge themselves with, but their own success will be without with.

Untitled #10

A breath of fresh air
whimsically there,

My fear of the known
familiar styles I cannot condone,

An inspiration taken from me
imitation seems to be the highest form of flattery.

<u>Mood Ring</u>

Red, white, black, blue or green,
colours that dictate my emotions,
like a mood ring that must be seen,
across the thousand billowing oceans.

Untitled #11

We stood there by the koi pond with our hearts content, baring all for the world to see. Stripping down the layers of life and pain, a feeling so wholesome though one part was hidden, I could not figure out.

When I finally looked deep into his eyes, I found a lie so hurtful and devastating that I just could not bear to be there with him anymore.

No right place nor right time, simply vanishing, a girl he no longer knows.

Her heart shattered

Shattering like the finest of china when she heard the
news. The flowers all around her fell like broken hues.

Though her plates were repaired with kintsugi
she looked beautiful, but it was all me, me, me.

Dark selfish desires consumed her very being,
taken by it all she was neither living nor seeing,

That great, big and beautiful world out there
was shattered all around her when she fell into despair.

<u>Forgive me.</u>

I'm sorry for the things
that I couldn't do for you,

I know I should have
been a lot more patient,

I just couldn't help it,
I had to let you go.

Stuck

I've never felt so suffocated,
in this country, in this state,
in this city, in this room.

Surrounded by people
that say they care,
but all I see is,
nothing.

I've never felt so suffocated,
where my feet, where my hands,
where my body, couldn't move.

Surrounded by people
that say they love,
but all I see is
the dark.

I've never felt so suffocated,
where in my head, in my mind,
in my soul, I couldn't make a change.

Surrounded by my thoughts
and trapped within them,
I'm stuck, in this country,
in this state, in this city
and in this room.

Oh, how I yearn to be under the stars far from the city with you.

Sweet Depression

Oh my sweet, sweet depression
what a sad companion you are,

You play and toil with my mind
and cheer tears from my head to the far,

You succumb to me and give me breaks
on those days that I win our spar,

But oh my sweet, sweet depression
a sad companion, that you are.

Untitled #12

Lilac coloured skies, an oceanic breeze
such a delight I thought, sitting next to you with ease.
Drinking your can of beer, the sun is setting
inside we go to begin our threading.

I know your heart was shattered when I ended things with you but I beg you to be hopeful, because in the sea there's room for two.

Untitled #13

On days like this, alone,
without further distractions,
standing tall, with smiles of gold,
you truly appreciate your surroundings.

The air so clean and the wind so warm,
you stop and smell the roses.

Longing

Oh how I long for a life outside the city, outside the noise, outside the stenches from machinery.

Far-far away from the millions of people, alone with my animal companions.

Oh how I long to be one with nature, one with peace, and a house and a garden on a thousand acres.

Far-far away from all the light pollution, to be alone with the stars at night.

Oh how I long to smell the forest every morning, lay by the lake and paint and write until the next morning.

Far-far away from the concrete jungle, alone just on my own.

Idea of You

I love the idea of you but
I don't think I can love you right now,
I'm sorry that I'm so broken,
my mind just never rests.

I wish

I wish I could let you love me
but my heart is split in two,
I hope that you can forgive me
because I'd like to be with you.

<u>Untitled #14</u>

To compete with the world around me
and the poets that write beautiful words like mine
is a fate that I've come to be with
as long as my future is fine.

Although I fear the many
talented beings around me
I long and hope for a world
where everyone enjoys poetry.

Oh, but you ran away didn't you baby,
you're now six feet under the ground.

Window

I sit there by the window waiting for you to come back,
I guess the loss hasn't settled yet, beating off the track.

I sit there writing poems, looking outside and in,
I guess the feelings I have are coming from within.

I sit there by my bed side praying to my God,
my calls unanswered these philosophies feel flawed.

I sit there brewing feelings, the dark begins to loom,
I guess these brewed out feelings feel the need to bloom.

I sit there by the window waiting for you to come back,
I know the loss has settled, because I know you won't be
back.

Untitled #15

I wish my mind would stop at once,
these heaving thoughts make me so blunt,
and brash, and emotional, but not thoughtful.

I make decisions that I'll soon regret,
but my mind wouldn't stop debilitating me,
I think to myself, oh how I'd love a cigarette.

I long for an escape from this punishing world,
even for a moment, in a way that will shorten,
my life on this unfair plain.

And I see her in the mirror, and cry out loud,
about how cruel this world can clearly be,
unforgiving and challenging to me.

I play a tune

I play a tune that's soft as sand,
I feel your pulse within my hand.

Coursing through your fallen arteries,
your soul kept within my heart's armouries.

The last note plays,
the last note fades,

in my heart your memory persuades.

Untitled #16

I lay alone at night and begin to forget,
our crazy adventures and all the mental letters.

The smell of paint, the canvas still wet,
I close my eyes in hopes to realise,

That my memories fade in time,
and that one day I will be fine.

You were meant to show me the world,
but now I'll have to see it all alone.

<u>Wait for me in Heaven</u>

So say yes to heaven
and wait there for me,

I promise to come
as soon as I'm free,

But I need to stay
here alone by the sea.

Untitled #17

For a long time I have felt like a fraud,
flirting with darkness my mind abroad.

I understand that I chose to live this way,
thank God the holy voice inside led me far away,

I'm glad it did as I'd not be the same,
working through my struggles and beating this game,

Though my far-flung hopes and dreams
were left as fractured crystal streams

I wondered if the things I wished for
were all that they seemed.

A poem to my future

I hold onto you like a toy from childhood,
cherished immensely like my old neighbourhood.

I journeyed far and wide across oceans and deserts to by
your side although memories only hold what the feeble
mind can store, the past traumas can be traced all the way
back to the war, and though you may see this as utter
nonsense, you can't refute that our lives are past tense.

As creatures of habit we fold and we grow, hoping that
one day we'd be able to show, the life we've lived up until
this point, to share with our grand-children whom we will
appoint the keepers of our legacies, their youthful mind
filled with jealousy of what we've done and whom we've
met they sit there imagining every step it took you to get
to that place, they sit there pondering at "What pace?",
they see pictures of your past lovers and friends,
they sit there wondering how did it all end.

The one thing that you keep from them, is all the hatred
and the pain that you endured from all the scum
things you'd never wish upon anyone.

As you grow older and fall with the flowers the treasures
you collected now give you powers in the afterlife that
you hope that's there, entering the gates all the way up in
the air greeted by the ones that loved you most and by
strangers that you could've known, almost.

Breeze In The Water

And though your bones lay inside the big blue marble
your little cherubs create a marvel they come and visit
every year lay down flowers and disappear,
They live their lives and prosper forth enveloped by your
watchful eye and your hopeful warmth.

They believe in themselves and attempted many
they struggled and they fought, just like you, deserving
plenty.

Stories they'll share with their own offspring,
leaving behind almost everything except the one thing
that they will miss taken too soon by a fateful kiss.

No longer there to give advice, no longer there to devise
a simple plan of sorts to help them along their journey of
course,

and when they grow old they'll wonder who they could've
been, I say this to my future grand-children,

"don't live in the past darling let yourself be seen".

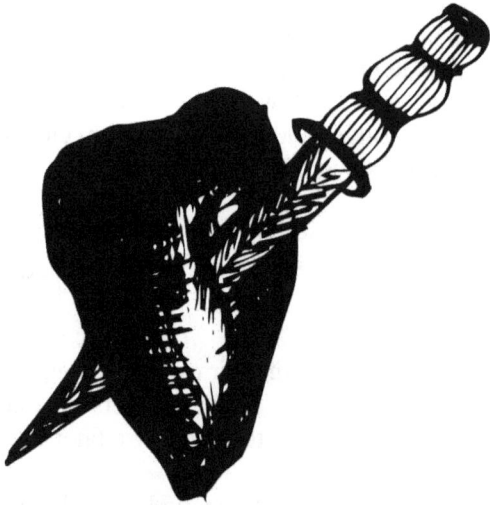

The only thing that truly hurts are the memories you left with me, they stab my heart almost daily until my eyes are left to bleed.

Kirribilli

I remember that day with you,
fresh in my mind like it was yesterday,
we walked the streets of Kirribilli
taking photos in the rain.

We walked along the water's edge
discussing things like we'd usually do.
I asked you if you would live here
you replied with "I would with you".

You sat on the edge overlooking the harbour,
looking so peaceful meditating by the water.
For a split second, I was worried that you'd jump
so I yelled and screamed and made a fuss.

Oh how well you put up with me
but now I'm lonely and you're nowhere to be seen.
We explored that neighbourhood
and dreamt up stories of how we'd live,

We ran through wind and rain
feeling like we were gyved,
we ran the way to Luna Park
under the harbour bridge,

We promised each other that
we would be back some day,
but now the suburb feels too deadly
for my heart to go astray.

<u>Dear John</u>

I'm unsure what to say to you
as my mind is plagued in many places,
but I hope that wherever you are
you're surrounded by warm familiar faces.

I miss your autumn sunrise hair,
with tints of copper everywhere,
I miss your touch and kisses too,
I miss your voice and everything about you.

I hope you knew that everyone loved you,
because we still cry knowing we're without you.
But the best we can do is carry on living
you touched our hearts and souls, forgiving.

You'll never be forgotten you see,
because I'll continue to write my poetry.
You're up there now looking down on us all,
blessing and praying that we don't fall.

I hope you see how wonderful life could be,
though you're not exactly here to witness it my dear.
I beg if you can please look down and protect me,
because I'm feeling scared without you here.

Oh my baby what a silly thing you've done
the sun now rises but we didn't have our fun.
Of course I can't hate you, you're at peace,
but within my heart now, I'm missing a piece.

Breeze In The Water

I hope that your heart and your mind feel free
I want to thank you for the lessons you taught me,
I often wondered what I'd learn from them
and now I live life growing from them.

You taught me a love that I didn't know existed,
faulted yet perfect, beautiful and untwisted.
Without you I would have never listened,
or learnt the feeling of being rechristened.

I now look to the sky and see your charming face,
I now sleep at night hoping that you'd visit every day
I now feel in a way that is closer to grace,
I miss you John dearly, I wished you'd have stayed.

I hope you rest my young sweet prince,
life was tough and feelings were held in.
Now close your eyes and rest awhile,
I'll see you up there in dreams within.

Our love wilted as quickly as it bloomed.

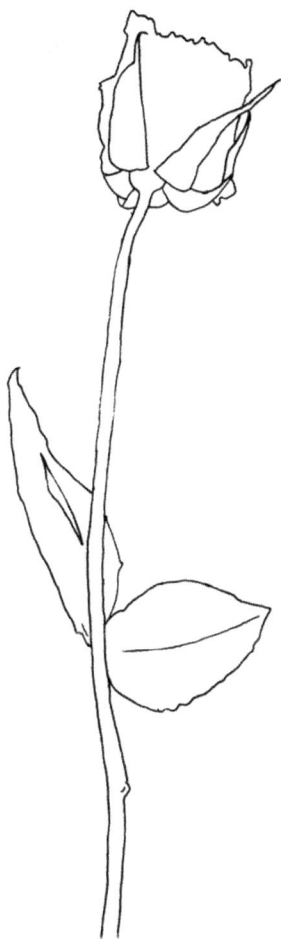

About the book

Breeze In The Water was published in November of 2019, the book touches upon the topics of trauma, loss, life, death, living, contemplation, passion, and all human emotion that present and define poetry and writing.

The initial concept was birthed in the southern hemisphere summer of 2015 whilst on holiday in the Great Barrier Reef. However as time progressed the book came into its own life and being, blooming into a representation of the experiences and feelings of the author over the past four-five years.

About the Author

Alexandra V. Tanygina is a poet, writer and multi-disciplinary artist born in the Mari-El Republic in Russia. She relocated with her mother to Australia at a young age and began to develop and grow her practices there.